CIRCUSES

CIRCUSES

Under the Big Top

by Judith Janda Presnall

A First Book

FRANKLIN WATTS
A DIVISION OF GROLIER PUBLISHING
New York   London   Hong Kong   Sydney
Danbury, Connecticut

For my husband, Lance

The author would like to thank 1994 Circus Vargas flying aerial artists Andrea and Katya Quiroga of the Flying Tabares from Buenos Aires, Argentina, and single trapeze performer Rebeca Perez from California for their interviews.

Photographs ©: Archive Photos: 2 (American Stock), 49; Art Resource/V & A Museum: 16; Bettmann Archive: 19, 34, 45; Circus World Museum, Baraboo, Wisconsin: 28, 30-31, 38, 47; Cirque Du Soleil/Dan Lavoie: 57; Comstock: 35, 42; Lloyd Fox: 10, 54, 58; North Wind Picture Archives: 15; Courtesy of Ringling Bros. and Barnum & Bailey Combined Shows, Inc.: cover, 9, 32, 50; Superstock, Inc.: 13, 22-23, 51; UPI/Bettmann: 24, 26, 40.

Library of Congress Cataloging–in–Publication Data

Presnall, Judith Janda.
    Circuses: under the big top / Judith Janda Presnall.
        p. cm.—(A First book)
    Includes bibliographical references and index.
    Summary: Describes how circuses got their start and what
is happening under the big top today.
    ISBN 0-531-20235-6 (lib.bdg.) ISBN 0-531-15808-x (pbk.)
    1. Circuses—Juvenile literature. [1. Circuses.] I. Title.
II. Series.
GV1817.P74   1996
791.3—dc20   96-15142
                                                        CIP
                                                        AC

Contents

THE CIRCUS COMES TO TOWN

The circus is coming! The circus is coming!" Since the early 1800s, the arrival of a circus in town has created excitement. Colorful posters, parades, and, later, sound trucks announced the coming event.

Some circuses floated on steamboats to ports all along the Mississippi and Ohio rivers. Others traveled in horse-drawn wagons. Their wooden wheels jolting over cobbled streets and through narrow, muddy country roads gave circuses the name **mud shows**

By the 1870s, some circuses journeyed by rail, thundering 50 to 100 miles (80 to 160 km) a night instead of the usual 15 to 20 miles (24 to 32 km) by wagon. In 1900, close to one hundred circuses entertained rural America. Today there are about fifty traveling circuses in the United States. The only one that still moves by train is the giant Ringling Brothers and Barnum & Bailey Combined Circus, which performs only in indoor arenas.

The three largest tented shows in the United States are Clyde Beatty Cole Brothers from Florida, Circus Vargas from California, and Carson & Barnes Wild Animals Circus from Oklahoma. Sites for tented circuses range from fairgrounds to ball fields to shopping-mall parking lots. Small circuses tour with trucks, trailers, and motor homes. Between March and October, they travel as many as 20,000 miles (32,190 km) and may appear in as many as one hundred cities.

Depending on the size of the circus, there can be a caravan of twenty to fifty trucks. Vehicles in a "rolling" circus include a generator truck, which supplies electric

A circus crowd gathers outside an early show tent.

Raising the
circus tent
is hard work
for elephant and man.

power, a ticket office on wheels, souvenir and animal trucks, a dormitory truck, the cookhouse, or **pie car**, equipment trucks, and motor homes. Tasks that must be handled ahead of time include buying food for circus personnel and animals, hooking up water, setting up rest rooms, hiring local laborers, repairing asphalt, and organizing lot cleanup.

Once on the lot, the circus crew must raise the tent. This impressive spectacle attracts crowds of people who delight in seeing elephants use brute strength to raise the one-ton center poles. The folded-and-wound striped canvas tent is unloaded from spool trucks. Workers lace it together manually and fasten it to steel rings on the center poles. After about four hours of work, the tent is finally erected. It must then be equipped with seats, or **lumber**, **ring curbs**, the big animal cage, props, lights, aerial equipment, and other show gear.

The circus could not function without its laborers, or **roustabouts**. Life in the circus is especially difficult for roustabouts. They often sleep in cramped quarters, perhaps four bunks high in a dormitory truck. They may clean themselves with water from a hose. They eat in a cook tent. They usually do not mix with townspeople. Some roustabouts stay on with the circus for the entire season. Others **blow the show** after a month, a week, or even days. On the positive side, many roustabouts enjoy the adventure of travel and visiting cities and towns in many states.

Being part of a circus, as a performer or as a crew member, is not easy. Life on the road requires traveling nine to eleven months a year with no time to make friends outside the circus. Home is usually nothing more than a parking area or a dirt lot. Circus members work from sunup to sundown. Four days a week, circus youngsters, or **punks**, spend three hours on schoolwork and two to three hours on circus training. They also take part in evening performances and do five shows on weekends.

Despite the rigors of circus life, these performers are devoted to their profession and their way of life. A common passion for the circus brings circus people together. Out on the road they often become as close as family.

Although much has changed since the first circuses came to town in horse-drawn wagons, circuses continue to entertain audiences with thrills, laughs, and wonder under the **big top**

For this trio of "punks," like many who work in the show, the circus is home.

BEFORE THE BIG TOP

The circus as we know it today has been passed along to us in bits and pieces. A feat that began in one country soon crossed boundaries to become worldwide.

Wall paintings portraying acrobats and balance artists were found in the Nile River valley of Egypt dating back as far as 2500 B.C., more than four thousand years ago. Palace murals, tiles from tombs, and temple carvings also pictured bull-leapers, jugglers, balancers, and trained monkeys.

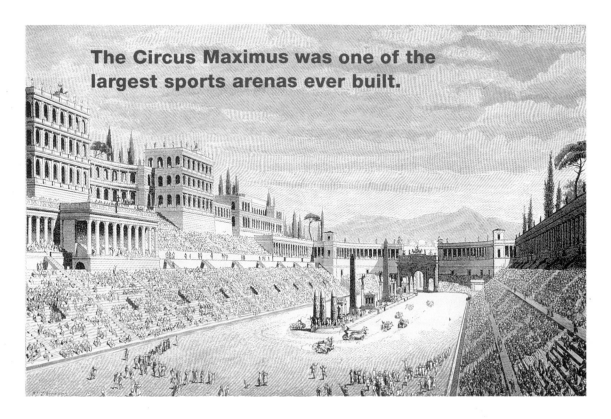

The Circus Maximus was one of the largest sports arenas ever built.

About 800 B.C., Greece gave us the mythical strong man Hercules, the world's first lion trainer, and the tradition of comic pantomime (performance without words). It also hosted the first competitive athletic games: chariot and horse races in oval tracks called hippodromes.

In Rome, circuses began around 329 B.C. with chariot races as the only event. Eventually other entertainment was added, including gladiators, boxers, wrestlers, elephant and camel races, and horse events. These shows were held in a horseshoe-shaped outdoor arena, with many rows of seats called the Circus Maximus. Expanded twice, it eventually seated 250,000 spectators and was the largest stadium of the time. Although chariot races for the 1959 movie *Ben Hur* were filmed there, the stadium now lies in decay. Our modern circus arenas are modeled after the Circus Maximus.

In A.D. 80, the Colosseum was built in Rome. Fifty thousand spectators could sit close to the action in this oval-shaped building. The Colosseum had a stitched canvas roof, making it the first big top.

During medieval times, musical entertainers called minstrels and troubadours traveled throughout Europe. At the end of the 1500s, England built permanent theaters or performance rings. At about the same time, a kind of Italian theater called commedia dell'arte, which is Italian for "comedy of art," was popularized. Our modern comedians and clowns grew out of this Italian tradition of ensemble acting.

This figure from the Italian commedia dell'arte was one of the world's original clowns.

The modern circus began in London in 1768 with a trick rider named Philip Astley. Astley combined acts of tumblers, jugglers, ropedancers, clowns, and horse shows into one entertainment and earned the name Father of the Circus. Astley also originated the standard 42-foot- (almost 13-m-) diameter circus ring still used today.

Some twenty years later, John Bill Ricketts, a Scottish horseman, opened a circus in America. Held in Philadelphia in April 1793 in a wooden amphitheater, the show attracted many distinguished guests, including President George Washington.

During the first eighty years of the American circus, equestrian acts dominated the show. Performances showed trick riders, riderless horses, and dancing horses, which are still seen at today's circuses. It wasn't long before wild animals were added to the circus.

Because the United States was mostly rural in the 1800s, circus owners departed from the European tradition of using permanent buildings and instead developed traveling shows. The number of owners soon increased when others realized they might make money by putting on a circus and tried their hand at it. In 1826, Nathan Howes and Aaron Turner presented their shows beneath a canvas tent, giving the American circus its own unique character.

Competition between circuses was fierce and there was much trading and combining of shows every season. One circus owner, Phineas T. Barnum, turned his operation into the richest and the biggest circus of the time. In 1881, Barnum joined with James Bailey. They called their combined circuses "The Greatest Show on Earth."

In 1870, five brothers from the Ringling family were given free passes to a circus in Iowa. After catching "circus fever," the brothers worked to obtain animals and performers and finally put on their own show twelve years later. Even though it was a financial and artistic disaster, they kept at it. By the end of the century, the Ringling brothers were the chief rival of the Barnum and Bailey Circus. In 1918, the two shows merged. The circus, which had begun as an intimate, one-ring performance in Europe, was transformed by Americans into a three-ring extravaganza.

During the golden age of the circus, from the 1870s until the 1920s, the parade, midway sideshows, and wild animals were all additional attractions that lured adults and children of all ages to the circus.

A poster from the early 1900s announces coming attractions.

THE GOLDEN AGE OF THE CIRCUS

In the early 1800s, circuses staged parades to announce their arrival in town. The circus parade was simple and quick.

At the edge of town, circus performers donned colorful clothes and feathered hats and marched through the streets. Trumpeters on horseback provided music.

When canvas tents became part of circus equipment and wagons were needed to transport them, things changed.

Before entering a new city, wagon drivers washed their horses and put on fancy clothes and circus members hung banners on the brightly painted vehicles. Then a small musical band climbed onto a wagon and the entertainment started.

As time passed, circus crews began going directly to their lots to set up their tents. They then put on a separate parade with wagons ornately carved and painted specially for the parade. Through the years, decorations on the wagons became more and more elaborate. They were trimmed with scrolls and borders, painted scenes, cupid statues, and thin layers of gold paint. Their webbed wheels made musical sounds as they moved down the street, adding to the gaiety of the parade.

Trying to outshine other shows, one large circus hitched up as many as forty horses to pull its lead bandwagon. Elephant herds marched trunk-to-tail single file down the street, wearing blankets that described the show as gigantic, tremendous, stupendous, or colossal. Sequin-costumed showgirls, clown wagons, caged exotic animals, decorated horses, and loud bands brought crowds rushing to the streets for a free glimpse of what was to come. A famous musical instrument, the calliope, brought up the tail end of the parade. This steam-run pipe organ's shrill whistle could be heard as far as 5 miles (8 km) away.

Because of increasing traffic problems, longer distances between lots and downtown parade areas, and soft asphalt roads that were unable to support heavy wagons, long parades—sometimes as long as a mile (1.6 km)—

Circus parades were colorful, noisy, and festive.

were eventually abandoned by the 1920s.

In their heyday, however, circus parades attracted thousands of people to the show grounds. Huge tents were topped with fluttering flags. Odors of hay, sawdust, and animals combined with the smells of hot dogs, popcorn, and cotton candy. Music and midway barkers peppered the ears of circus-goers.

It was the midway barker's job to lure curious people to buy tickets to the midway tents, where curiosities, sideshows, and other amusements were located. "Step right up, folks. Step in a little closer!" he shouted over and over. Inside the midway tents, ticket buyers might see a giant, a midget, a tattooed lady, a snake charmer, a sword swallower, a fire-eater, or conjoined

A 1914 circus parade makes its way down Main Street.

twins. Those who agreed to be exhibited took great pride in earning a living this way. Today, however, sideshows are mostly a thing of the past. After viewing the sideshow, circus-goers could use their general admission ticket to enter the menagerie, or wild animal tent.

In the 1930s, rivalry between American showmen was so intense that circus owners traveled to India or Africa in search of unusual attractions for their menageries. They brought back exotic animals, including giraffes, hippopotamuses, lions, snakes, gorillas, and even a sacred white elephant. For many circus-goers, it was the first time they had ever seen these animals. Dozens of wagons displayed caged Bengal tigers, jaguars, kangaroos, and chimpanzees. Chained or tethered in tents, camels, llamas, zebras, and the popular elephants were an impressive sight up close.

Unfortunately, some circuses offered more than unusual animals, superb performers, and delicious food and pink lemonade. From the 1860s to the 1920s, many thieves roamed circus grounds. One circus showman, Adam Forepaugh, was noted for hiring professional pickpockets "to work the crowd." Forepaugh even hired a blind lady to beg for money, 90 percent of which went into his pocket. High ticket windows made it difficult for circus customers to count change and easy for sellers to cheat them.

If a circus was found to be operating dishonestly, townspeople ran them out of the area and forbade their return. In order to protect their image, honest circuses tried to control their workers with rules of conduct. Circuses without problems became known as **Sunday school shows**. Ringling Brothers and Barnum & Bailey led the way. Entertainment in honest, safe surroundings for the whole family became the goal of most circuses.

A showman drives a circus cart pulled by a harnessed hippo.

FOUR

ANIMAL ACTS

Lions, tigers, elephants, horses, bears, gorillas, camels, giraffes, zebras, chimpanzees, and even dogs have played important roles in the circus. These mostly wild animals, however, are trained, not tamed. While early animal trainers punished animals to make them obedient, modern-day trainers prefer kinder methods.

In 1917, Alfred Court, a Frenchman, was one of the first to train big cats (lions and tigers) with compassion and patience. Before training wild animals, Court made friends

The first famous female cat trainer, Mabel Stark, romps with a tiger.

with them. He would enter the training ring with a leather pouch full of beef. Offering the meat on the end of a sharp stick, he talked to the animal, slowly moved closer, and soon would be stroking it. As part of his act, he even planted a kiss on the muzzle of a tiger.

The first famous female cat trainer was Mabel Stark. From the age of eight, when she saw her first circus, she longed to step into a cage with the big cats. Later, as a circus performer, Stark entered the cage unarmed and directed her big cats by speaking softly and signaling with her arms and legs. The 114-pound (52-kg) performer wrestled with Bengal tigers and taught them to ride atop horses. At the end of her act, she placed her head into a tiger's mouth. Although working with the ferocious animals often left Stark mangled, clawed, and bitten, she always returned immediately to the cage as soon as she healed.

Another American performer, Clyde Beatty, also believed no jungle animal could be trained successfully by cruelty. Beatty was a superb entertainer who could make people think he was in danger even though his show was harmless. In his 1925 act, he staged what looked like a fierce battle between man and beast. Beatty crouched, poked chairs toward the tigers, cracked his whip, and occasionally fired his blank-filled pistol. Although Beatty

Clyde Beatty astounded audiences by performing in the cage with jungle animals.

rarely placed himself in real danger, the noise and antics combined with the roar of forty tigers and lions presented a suspenseful spectacle.

A member of the Ringling show since 1968, Gunther Gebel-Williams has earned the title of The Greatest-Ever Animal Trainer in the World. An animal lover since childhood, Gebel-Williams began his circus career in West Germany at the age of twelve. His ability to work with animals came from his devotion to them. Gebel-Williams spent many hours every day feeding, petting, and talking to them. Throughout his career, he has always worked with his tigers as a trainer, not a tamer. Although Gebel-Williams retired from performing in 1990, he still travels with the Ringling show as a manager.

Elephants, one of the most popular circus attractions, are considered to be the most intelligent of circus animals.

A tiger stands on two legs at the command of its trainer, Gunther Gebel-Williams.

Elephants can be trained to respond to up to twenty-seven commands. They have been the stars of parades and circuslike performances for over four thousand years. Most are sweet tempered and develop a loyal affection for their caretakers. Elephant performers are usually female but they are all called bulls. In the show ring, elephants balance on a tiny tub and make pyramids by putting their forefeet on each other's backs. Sometimes they wrap their trunk around performers and lift them in the air.

One of the first elephants to come to the United States arrived in New York harbor from London around 1804. A shrewd Yankee showman, Hachaliah Bailey, brought the gray-trunked African mammal to his home in Somers, New York. For the next thirteen years, Bailey showed Old Bet in most of the small towns of New England and New York. He traveled in the dark of the night so folks along the way would be unable to get a free peek at the curious creature from across the sea. A statue of Old Bet is a landmark at the old Elephant Hotel in Somers, which now houses a circus museum.

The most famous elephant of all time was Jumbo, which P. T. Barnum bought from the London Zoo in 1882 for his circus. The largest and heaviest elephant in captivity at the time, Jumbo was 11 feet (3.4 m) high, 14 feet (4.3 m) long, and weighed almost 7 tons (6,350 kg). At

Jumbo was brought to the United States in 1882.

one time, Jumbo's skeleton was mounted in New York City's American Museum of Natural History.

Performing horses and performers are another favorite animal act of the circus. Performers ride bareback, completing impressive acrobatic feats on one or more galloping horses. Trick horsemanship was first introduced into the ancient Roman circus by stuntmen who rode standing on two horses, with one foot on the back of each horse. Called Roman riding, this stunt is still popular. Horses that appear in circuses fall into three categories: rosinbacks, liberty horses, and Lipizzaners.

Rosinbacks are sturdy animals with broad backs to carry bareback riders and acrobats. Rosinbacks are so named because their backs are sprinkled with rosin dust to give performers a surer footing.

Liberty horses are horses that perform riderless, reinless, and without restraint, displaying freedom and independence. Performing in groups of six to twelve, liberty horses trot in circles, do reverse turns, and stand on their hind legs.

The aristocrats of the circus-ring horses are the pure white Lipizzaners, which are an actual breed. Only stallions perform the classic dance steps, side

A Lipizzaner stallion performs with help from its trainers.

steps, high-stepping cakewalks, upright twirls, and graceful bows, known as dressage. The horses are cued by hand signals or verbal commands from their trainers.

Some equestrian families have been working in circuses for nearly a century. These families include the Cristianis, who perform a comedy act with horses, and the Loyals, who are famous for their seven-person pyramid atop five galloping horses.

SKY-HIGH STUNTS

Trapeze, tightrope, and acrobatic performances are some of the circus' most thrilling and suspenseful events. The aerialist's tricks include leaping from a trapeze suspended high above the ground, balancing on a tightrope stretched sky-high across the circus tent, and juggling flaming objects.

The circus performer, or **kinker**, regularly attempts these daring and dangerous feats in front of live audiences. Skilled kinkers have come from all over the world.

Antoinette Concello flies through the air on her trapeze.

Before the mid-1800s, trapeze acts consisted of flyers leaping from one ground-based bar to another. In Toulouse, France, Jules Léotard practiced by hanging two trapeze bars over the swimming pool in his father's gymnasium. In 1859, after nine years of training, Léotard staged his first aerial performance at Paris's Cirque Napoléon. He was wearing a new, skintight one-piece costume, which now bears his name. Both the tights and the performance stimulated immediate interest and excitement.

Flyers in Europe and America then began performing single and double aerial somersaults. By 1870, another performer called a catcher was added to the second bar. The catcher has the important job of being there at the right time to catch the flyer safely. The triple somersault, known as the big trick, soon followed. In 1937, Antoinette Concello became the first woman to perform the triple somersault and was billed as The World's Greatest Woman Aerialist.

Trapeze artistry requires many skills, including discipline, precision, grace, and timing. One spectacular trick is the passing leaps that involve two flyers in the air at the same time. Forward somersaults and pirouettes, or body twirls, are particularly dangerous tricks since the flyers cannot see their target until the last minute.

Male and female performers on the single hanging trapeze and the double rings use no safety net. They, however, will sometimes wear a wide belt called a mechanic attached to a safety cable to catch them in the event of a fall.

Today, Mexicans are the most respected flying trapeze artists. This honor dates all the way back to the early 1900s and Alfredo Codona, who was considered the greatest trapeze artist of his time. His act was a nonstop blur of triple somersaults and double pirouette returns. Codona was married to another aerialist—the Queen of the Air, Lillian Leitzel.

A high-wire artist makes his way across a baseball stadium while thousands of spectators look on.

Leitzel earned her fame flying through the air suspended by a rope loop. Without a safety net, Leitzel performed acrobatic moves such as knee and ankle hangs, splits, twirls, and headstands. The most exciting part of Leitzel's performance was her revolutions at the peak of the tent. After slipping her wrist into a swivel loop of rope, Leitzel propelled her tiny body up and around while the hypnotized spectators counted her spinning turns to a drumroll. Her record was 249 twirls. In 1931, Leitzel fell to her death after her rigging broke during a performance.

Tightrope performances can be just as suspenseful as flying trapeze acts. The great tightrope walkers, or funambulists, have traditionally come from Germany. Walking on a suspended rope, however, was first popularized by a Frenchman who used the name Blondin in the 1800s. Blondin, unaffiliated with any circus, thrilled crowds with his high-wire walks across Niagara Falls in 1859.

In current high-wire acts, ropes have been replaced by steel strands tightly wound into $\frac{5}{8}$-inch (1.6-cm) cables. Wire acts in the circus include: (1) the slack wire, which sways easily and is suitable for clowning; (2) the bounding wire, which has springs at one or both ends that permit somersaulting; and (3) the high and low tightwires, upon which performers use a parasol (an elegant umbrella) for balance.

Adding performers on the tightrope adds risk. One popular high-wire family, the Wallendas, came to America from Germany in 1928. Their seven-person, three-layer pyramid, first performed in 1947, made them famous. The daring team, linked by shoulder bars, stepped slowly and carefully from one end of the wire to the other while spectators held their breath. The Wallenda family performed this human pyramid act for fifteen years. Sadly, during a performance in 1962, two members of the team were killed. Today, several Wallendas continue to perform high-wire acts.

Closer to the ground, acrobatic stunts have grown in popularity. Once sideshow attractions, this kind of circus entertainment has moved to the main tent in modern circuses. Acts include leapers and vaulters, tumblers, and acrobatic troupes. The Chinese are generally recognized as the world's best acrobats.

Other ground performers include acrobats called contortionists, who twist their bodies into extraordinary positions, and jugglers, who keep beanbags, flaming sticks, knives, and bowling balls in the air. In a performance called a Risley act, jugglers lie on their backs and balance or juggle people with their feet.

During all these trapeze, tightrope, and acrobatic acts, circus audiences experience a range of emotions. They hold their breath, they sigh with relief, and they cheer with delight. To lessen anxiety between these breathtaking stunts, the clowns take the stage to divert the audience with laughter.

A team of tumblers flip through the air and stack themselves on one another's shoulders.

CLOWN ALLEY

Laughter is good for the soul. The merriment of clowning has existed in every culture since the beginning of time. From medieval times, European kings and queens were entertained by court jesters. The jester's costume included a cap and long-toed slippers decorated with bells.

These bells jangled as he danced, juggled, performed acrobatics, pantomimed, and told riddles for his royal audiences. The Harlequin character, popular in Europe in the 1500s, wore a bandit's black mask and multicolored diamond-patterned tights with a white ruffled collar. He blended wisecracks and clever tricks with acrobatics.

A couple of centuries later, a man who never set foot in a circus became the inspiration for all clowns that followed. Born in London in 1778, Joseph Grimaldi played the role of a chained monkey in his father's pantomime act until the age of ten. Grimaldi later created the modern clown during a London pantomime. He painted his face white and applied a wide red mouth and designs on his face. As a final touch, Grimaldi added clusters of blue hair to his bald head and put on a ruffle-trimmed shirt and baggy breeches with deep pockets for hiding strings of sausages and live geese. Clowns are still called Joeys in honor of Joseph Grimaldi and his comic influence.

Joseph Grimaldi contributed greatly to the development of the modern clown.

45

The king of American clowns was Dan Rice. His costume of red-, white-, and blue-striped tights, a top hat, and chin whiskers is said to have been the model for Uncle Sam, the character that symbolizes the United States. Rice first appeared in Galena, Illinois, in 1844. This quick-witted, charming clown teased audience members, talked about politics, and recited silly facts and poetry to laughing crowds.

With the establishment of three-ring circuses and big tops, audiences had trouble hearing the clowns' spoken humor. This reality resulted in new, silent clowns and a uniquely American style of clowning. Performers wore colorful wigs and flamboyant costumes with big, floppy shoes. They used exaggerated body language, loud noises, and oversized props to create foolish routines that made their audiences roar with laughter.

There are three types of modern clowns: whiteface, auguste, and character. Whiteface clowns cover their face entirely in white makeup and add colorful designs. Wearing clothes that they design themselves, whiteface clowns act as the straight man, setting up gags for other clowns to complete.

Felix Adler was a famous whiteface grotesque clown, which meant he had a white face with oversized features like a large red mouth and enlarged eyes. Adler had a big

Whiteface grotesque performer Felix Adler clowns.

supply of jeweled false noses, some of which lit up. He wore lavishly padded clothes around the hips to appear oversized. Adler even used trained piglets and a mule in his comic routine.

Auguste clowns are less refined and less skilled than the whiteface clowns. Auguste clowns use light-colored makeup to outline the eyes and mouth generously in white and then add features in red and black. These clowns wear loose-fitting clothes for tumbling, falling, and slapstick routines, purposely making mistakes throughout the act.

One legendary auguste clown was Lou Jacobs. He became famous for creating the world's tiniest car and folding his 6-foot (1.8-m) frame into it. Jacobs's faithful pal, a Chihuahua dog named Knucklehead, was part of his act for fourteen years.

Character clowns often have black beards and white mouths and wear tattered, tramplike clothes. Playing childlike, sad, and down-on-their luck characters, these clowns usually work alone.

Emmett Kelly was a well-known character clown. He portrayed the never-smiling miserable tramp Willie. Kelly's most famous routine was an earnest attempt at sweeping spotlights off the floor. The foolishness of the task kept spectators in stitches.

Emmett Kelly popularized the "tramp" character clown.

Clowns are the glue that hold a circus show together. They first appear in the **come-in** while audience members are finding their seats. They also **bust out** between acts, perform in **walk-arounds**, and have a spotlighted skit.

Before they perform, clowns get ready in an area or tent called clown alley, set up solely for their use. During a show, this common dressing room is a place of great disorder and confusion. In clown alley, there are usually long rows of tables littered with tubes of greasepaint, cold cream, wigs, putty noses, costumes, props, and other clowning supplies. A clown's face and costumes are considered personal property and cannot be copied.

Clown alley buzzes with activity before and during show time.

A Joey busts out with his furry sidekick.

Classes to learn the art of clowning are offered at universities throughout the United States. The Ringling Brothers and Barnum & Bailey Clown College, in Baraboo, Wisconsin, has been teaching how to clown since 1968. In an eight-week session, students learn slapstick, unicycle riding, mime, juggling, acrobatics, stilt walking, prop and costume construction, and makeup. A long tradition of male-only clowns was broken in 1970 when the first female clown, Peggy Williams, graduated from the Ringling Clown College.

A clown relies on surprise, exaggeration, magic, and slapstick to make audiences laugh. Through clever skits that seem to mimic life, clowns communicate happiness, pain, anger, fear, and bashfulness without using the spoken word. A respected club of highly trained and creative entertainers, these Joeys are devoted to bringing joy to others.

ONE-RING CIRCUSES

One-ring shows are modeled after the small circuses of Europe. Their concern is with the art of performance rather than lavish spectacle.

The best part of one-ring circuses is the friendly, up-close view. A curbside spectator can be dusted with sawdust, be sprayed with the saliva of racing horses, smell the animals, see the beaded sweat of intensely concentrated performers, and even watch a trapeze act from

A whiteface clown blows fire.

beneath the net. All viewers are no more than the width of a tennis court from the action.

Each circus works differently. Some supply the costumes and music and equipment for performers. Others "hire an act," which means that the performers supply everything themselves. One Argentine trapeze family from Circus Vargas, for example, designs and sews their own costumes. They also hand-stitch hundreds of sequins, a chore that can take up to three months.

Circus Vargas began its one-ring show in 1969. It removed animals from the show in 1994. During the season, performers work two or three shows a day, seven days a week. Besides working in the circus thirty-five weeks from March to November, most of the performers work during the off-season to keep their bodies in shape and to earn money.

The Pickle Family Circus is very small—about twenty-five people. This circus is run as a cooperative, which means that a performer may unload and pack trucks, run cables for lights, and make props in addition to performing in several different acts. A trampolinist, for example, may also do acrobatic tricks, juggling, and clowning. "Pickle" people live in tents. Their show takes place out in the open air, with bleachers and a **sidewall** around them.

When the gates open and the crowd surges toward the tent to find their seats, members of New York's Big Apple Circus are ready to put on a polished, highly professional show. The seventy-five member group travels from town to town in thirteen yellow tractor-trailers filled with props and equipment, three vans of animals, and a caravan of mobile homes.

In today's Big Apple Circus, the **ringmaster** and the leading lady equestrian are married. Paul Binder and Katja Schumann have two children, who are part of the horse act. Katja's father is also an equestrian performer with the group, making it a three-generation performance. Some performers never leave their families as one generation follows another in the circus life, and they continue to travel together.

One unique tent production is Le Cirque du Soleil, which is French for "circus of the sun." This French Canadian nonanimal circus has gained popularity since it started in 1984 in Montreal. The nonstop show is almost like a Broadway musical, dazzling its spectators with stunning costumes, colored smoke that floods the ring, swirling lights, and jazzy music. Le Cirque du Soleil combines daring human feats and high-tech theatrics in a dark, eerie setting. Twenty-five hundred spectators, sitting in a blue-and-yellow-striped tent, are transported into an exciting make-believe world.

Inspired by the Chinese circus, this one-ring show features gutsy, highly trained people recruited from around the world, some as young as seven years old. The show's spectacular feats have included fourteen riders on one bicycle and a team of four acrobats balancing on a zigzagging tower of chairs, as well as contortionists, trapeze artists, gymnasts, mimes, and clowns.

For Cirque du Soleil performers, the continued physical training and practice is difficult. They must commit to daily workouts, rehearsals three times a week, and a preshow warm-up. When a new show is being developed, performers practice fourteen hours a day for nine months. The show then goes on the road for eighteen months.

One-ring circuses are small in comparison to the Ringling Brothers extravaganzas,

Contemporary clowns strike a pose at Le Cirque du Soleil.

**Circus-goers grab a snack at the end of
a long day of fun under the big top.**

which have as many as five hundred people traveling in
two separate shows within the United States. Circuses
have become international shows, blending many talented
performers from different parts of the world. Large or
small, each circus takes pride in providing the best avail-
able talent.

Whether it's the smell of sawdust, performing animals, spectacular costumes and lights, or wondrous performers, the circus has something for everyone. So step
right up, get your popcorn and cotton candy, and enjoy
the magic under the big top.

CIRCUS TERMS

big top — tent used for the main circus performance

blow the show — to leave or quit

bust out — to enter the arena abruptly with other circus performers; usually refers to clowns

clown alley — the clowns' dressing area

come-in — the period of time, usually an hour, between when the circus gates are opened and the start of the show

kinker — any seasoned circus performer. The name originated from tumblers who worked the kinks out of sore muscles after exercise.

lumber — seats or bleachers

mud show — a small tented circus that travels overland but not by train

pie car — a dining car on a circus train, or a truck or tent that supplies food

punk — any circus youngster, human or animal

ring curb — curved pieces of wood that fit together to form a circus ring

ringmaster—the circus master of ceremonies

roustabout—a circus laborer who erects and disassembles tents, looks after the grounds, and cares for animals and equipment

sidewall—a canvas tent wall surrounding the bleachers to prevent passersby from seeing the show; to sneak past these walls during a performance without paying admission

Sunday school show—an honest circus; that is, one with no illegal activity

walk-around—a procession of clowns around the circus ring

FOR FURTHER READING

Carter, Kyle. *Circus Stars*. Vero Beach, Fla.: Rourke Press, 1994.

Cushman, Kathleen. *Circus Dreams: The Making of a Circus Artist*. Boston: Little, Brown, 1990.

Fleming, Alice. *P. T. Barnum: The World's Greatest Showman*. New York: Walker, 1993.

Krementz, Jill. *A Very Young Circus Flyer*. New York: Dell, 1987.

Machotka, Hana. *The Magic Ring: A Year with the Big Apple Circus*. New York: William Morrow, 1988.

Meyer, Charles R. *How to Be a Juggler*. New York: David McKay, 1977.

Stolzenberg, Mark. *Be a Clown*. New York: Sterling, 1989.

INDEX

Page numbers in *italics* indicate illustrations.

Judith Janda Presnall grew up in Milwaukee, Wisconsin. She has a bachelor's degree in education from the University of Wisconsin in Whitewater. A former teacher, she now devotes her time to writing for children. Ms. Presnall is the author of several children's books, including Franklin Watts's *Animal Skeletons* and *Animals That Glow,* which was named an outstanding science trade book for children by the National Science Teachers Association. She has received awards from the Society of Children's Book Writers & Illustrators and the California Writers Club for her children's nonfiction.

Judith Janda Presnall lives in southern California, with her husband, Lance. They have two grown children, Kaye and Kory.